Book 2 Pip and the Flyaway Balloon

It is Pip's birthday soon.
She wants to invite all...

PIP AND BUNNY: THE FLYAWAY BALLOON

The invaluable 'Pip and Bunny' collection is a set of six picture books with an accompanying handbook and e-resources carefully written and illustrated to support the development of visual and literary skills. By inspiring conversation and imagination, the books promote emotional and social literacy in the young reader.

Designed for use within the early years setting or at home, each story explores different areas of social and emotional development. The full set includes:

- six beautifully illustrated picture books with text and vocabulary for each
- a handbook designed to guide the adult in using the books effectively
- 'Talking Points' relating to the child's own world
- 'What's the Word?' picture pages to be photocopied, downloaded or printed for language development
- detailed suggestions as to how to link with other EYFS areas of learning.

The set is designed to be used in both individual and group settings. It will be a valuable resource for teachers, SENCOs (preschool and reception), Early Years Staff (nursery, preschool and reception), EOTAs, Educational Psychologists, Counsellors and Speech Therapists.

Maureen Glynn has 25 years' experience teaching primary and secondary age children in mainstream, home school and special school settings, in the UK and Ireland.

First published 2020
by Routledge
2 Park Square, Milton Park, Abingdon, Oxon OX14 4RN

and by Routledge
52 Vanderbilt Avenue, New York, NY 10017

Routledge is an imprint of the Taylor & Francis Group, an informa business

British Library Cataloguing-in-Publication Data
A catalogue record for this book is available from the British Library

Library of Congress Cataloging-in-Publication Data
A catalog record for this book has been requested

ISBN: 978-0-367-18905-1 (pbk)
ISBN: 978-0-429-35494-6 (ebk)

Typeset in Calibri
by Apex CoVantage, LLC

Visit www.Routledge.com/9780367136642

her nursery friends.

'Please come to my picnic party in the park. Pip.'

Her family...
parents, uncles, aunties and cousins...

and her four grandparents.

On the day,
Mummy and Daddy and grandparents
help to set up Pip's picnic party.

Pip says 'Hello' to everyone.

They have fun together and...

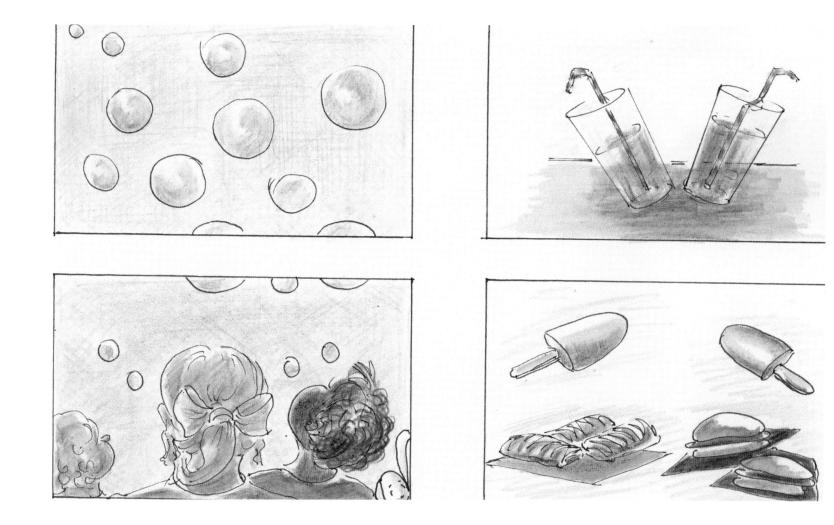

Pip blows out her birthday candles. But...

Tommy unties one of the balloons.

Oh! The wind is suddenly strong...

The balloon flies up high.
Higher and higher it goes.

'Where will it fly to, Bunny?' says Pip.

Book 2 The Flyaway Balloon What's the Word?

Show the page and ask the child to say words that explain each image:

Page 15 Action Words?

Page 16 Location Words?

Page 17 Birthday Words?

Page 18 Family/Relationship Words?

Page 19 Emotions and Feelings?

Action Words?

Location Words?

Birthday Words?

Family/Relationship Words?

Emotions and Feelings?